THE PRACTICAL GUIDE TO FREE SPEECH

THE COMMON-SENSE GUIDE TO THE FIRST
AMENDMENT

PRACTICAL GUIDES
BOOK 4

TOM MCHALE

Tom McHale
PRACTICAL GUIDES

CONTENTS

INTRODUCTION: WHY FREE SPEECH MATTERS

Let's play the *Twilight Zone* game.

Imagine a world where your neighbor could toss you in jail for an off-color joke (even if it were funny), or perhaps for posting an inappropriate meme, or a rant about your political point of view.

The world, for much of human history, was that *Twilight Zone*. The First Amendment is what makes America... well, America.

Let's open this discussion by noting free speech isn't just about talking; it's about thinking, debating, and keeping the powerful honest. For one example, if we can't criticize our own government, we're not really free, are we?

If you're looking for a simple cheat sheet, with a list of modern-day potential free speech transgressions and my opinion on whether or not the First Amendment protects them, you're in the wrong place; you won't find that here. You will find some checklists, but they're geared toward helping you consider the stakes set by the designers and major court decisions, not my personal opinions.

Instead, we're going to serve you much better. Rather

than delivering a fish for dinner, we're going to teach you "how to fish" by going through the thinking behind the concept of "freedom of speech."

When complete, you'll have a thorough understanding of the history, the underlying arguments, and the landmark cases that have helped refine the First Amendment's application to daily life. We'll also provide you with an overview of how freedom of speech applies in both public and private domains (again, as ruled by the courts over time), as well as instances where free speech has been limited. Think of wars and times of national distress.

We'll include a chapter talking about situations that obviously aren't examples of free speech and explain why. That section will be fun, but I promise, we'll tactfully remain outside of personal opinion territory and limit the discussion to concepts with clear and unambiguous factual support. Of course, you're free to disagree with the court cases that may have formed those ideas. That would be a very American approach and a great example of you exercising your right to free speech!

Near the end of all this, we'll spend some time talking about modern challenges that make freedom of speech arguments even more complicated. Social media, artificial intelligence, and new means of communication never fail to uncover new brain-twisting debates on free speech.

When all this is done, you'll be armed with the knowledge and context to understand free speech issues. But don't worry, we'll have fun along the way.

After reading this short book, you'll never watch the nightly news the same way again.

CHAPTER 1
THE "SIMPLE" PART

Of all the professions I considered from age five on, one that never entered my "danger close" radar range was "contract lawyer." Four out of five doctors agree that reading those causes Exploding Head Syndrome. That's a real condition, by the way, but thankfully limited to perceived sound in your head, not brain rattling explosions. OK, I'm kidding about contract law causing that, but I think we can all (possibly excepting you lawyers out there) agree it's a painful and tedious experience. Whereas, notwithstanding, indemnification, subrogation, Prima facie, Amicus curiae... You get the idea.

Thankfully, the First Amendment of the United States Constitution never would have cleared the bar to become a contract example in law school. At just 45 words, it's far shorter than your last McDonald's receipt. And, icing on the cake, it's easy to understand.

Here it is in its entirety:

 "Congress shall make no law respecting an establishment of religion, or prohibiting the free exercise

thereof; or abridging the freedom of speech, or of the press; or the right of the people peaceably to assemble, and to petition the Government for a redress of grievances."

That's it. No fine print. No sections or subsections. Just one slightly long sentence.

Yet these two score plus a couple of words have been responsible for more arguments, lawsuits and talk show debates than you can shake a gavel at.

Think about that for a second. Entire industries like broadcast media, print and online journalism, comedy, protests, talk shows, and many, many more depend on these forty-five words.

While it seems simple and its meaning obvious, the real-life details have kept legions of lawyers, judges and media commentators gainfully employed for well over 200 years.

Who's Actually Being Told "No"

Let's start with the obvious: the First Amendment begins by telling Congress what it cannot do. "Congress shall make no law..." is about as clear as it gets. A six-term politician can understand that.

Now, onwards and upwards.

Slow down for this part, as it becomes important later in the discussion. It doesn't say your boss, your homeowners association, the stranger on Facebook who keeps you up late at night posting stupid (and wrong) things. Right off the bat, it clearly applies to the government. The government cannot... (we'll get into more of what they cannot do shortly).

Like the rest of the Constitution and Bill of Rights, at

first, this target was painted squarely on the federal govern-ment. It was much later, with the passage and ratification of the 14th Amendment in 1868, that the process of applying bits and pieces of the Constitution and Bill of Rights to the states began.

And it was gradual. Starting in the 1920s, the Supreme Court started to address Constitutional provisions and make them enforceable at the state level, too, one by one. The First Amendment was incorporated at the state level, meaning the "shall make no law" part became enforceable in 1925 as part of the Gitlow v. New York case. Let's put that one on the back burner for now; we'll talk about Gitlow later in the chapter covering major case law events.

So, technically, prior to this, states could pretty much do what they wanted with respect to free speech.

Here's the takeaway for this "who's being told no" part. Suppose you say something weird or objectionable, and anyone besides the government penalizes you, like kicking you out of the Taco Bell after you tell waiting patrons the food is lousy and they shouldn't order. In that case, you can't whine about your constitutional right to free speech. You do have a right to free speech, but Taco Bell has the right to throw you out. So, don't insult the manager, thinking the First Amendment protects you.

What Counts as "Speech"?

Hmm. What is speech?

What we reproduced earlier is the entire text of the First Amendment. If you're paying attention, you'll note there is no definition of "speech" included. As a result, the courts have filled in the blanks in various cases over the years, ruling on what types of things are and are not examples covered under the term "speech."

Here are some examples:

The written word (pen and paper or electronic)? Protected.

Wearing a black armband in protest? Protected. (Tinker v. Des Moines, 1969). A school board tried to ban the move, but the protest was deemed free speech.

Burning an American flag? Protected (Texas v. Johnson, 1989). Flag burning was ruled to be a type of symbolic political speech, even if it offends other people. From the ruling: "If there is a bedrock principle underlying the First Amendment, it is that the government may not prohibit the expression of an idea simply because society finds the idea offensive or disagreeable."

Spending money on political ads? Protected (Citizens United v. FEC, 2010). In a conflict between the then-current election law and corporate and similar entities spending money on political content, the court ruled that spending money on political messaging is protected.

As for non-speaking roles like burning flags and shouting offensive things, related activities, like setting a car on fire with that burning flag, or punching your debate opponent in the nose, don't count as free speech expression. Yes, it gets sticky, and the courts have handled plenty of cases where they had to separate the expression of an idea from physical acts that may cause harm.

So "speech" in legal terms covers a lot of ground, but it's not a license to do anything you want and then claim you were just expressing yourself.

Free Speech Myths

Let's get you all riled up by touching on some common free speech myths. As the book progresses, we'll get into the details that will show the underlying framework defining why these common scenarios are myths.

"The First Amendment gives me the right to say whatever I want!"

Well, almost. You can get away with quite a bit (remember, we're talking about the government not being able to limit your speech), but you can't "say" or "express" just anything. You can't threaten or speak libelously or incite violence, for example.

"Free speech means I can speak my mind at work without getting fired."

This one is just flat out wrong. Remember, the First Amendment protects you from the government, not your employer. If you work at that Taco Bell we mentioned, you can't answer the phone, "Thanks for calling Taco Bell. I really prefer Taco Emporium, their food is much better and you should go there," even if you believe it. A lot of people miss the boat on this one when professional athletes protest while at work. It's legally up to their employers whether or not they can do that while on the job. If the employer allows it, then no problem!

Similarly, if your company has a policy about online conduct and you ignore it, your boss can show you the door. The Constitution doesn't come to work with you, at least in the case of the First Amendment.

"Social media censorship violates free speech."

A bit similar to the last myth, the social media overlords are private companies, so they can set their own rules. They can choose whether to show or not show their customers' content. However, should the government try to compel that company to silence certain views, then we might be talking about a First Amendment issue.

"You can't yell fire in a crowded theater."

Don't worry, we're going to gloss over this for now and come back to it in depth later.

The phrase comes from Justice Oliver Wendell Holmes in Schenck v. United States (1919). What he actually said was, "The most stringent protection of free speech would not protect a man in falsely shouting fire in a theatre and causing a panic."

Guess what? That case logic referencing clear and present danger has been replaced. A newer case, Brandenburg v. Ohio (1969), ruled that speech is only unprotected if it incites imminent lawless action. Unless your words are about to trigger a violent riot right now, they're probably protected. Of course, the theater owner could toss you on the street for yelling in the theater.

Why Start Here?

We're going to get into a lot more depth behind these high-level concepts, but don't worry; we're still going to have fun doing it. It's just crucial to get the words themselves straight first.

While it's short and sweet, the First Amendment is a compass. Once you know who it restrains, what counts as speech, and what myths to ignore, the rest of the journey through free speech history makes a lot more sense.

Most people don't complete a jigsaw puzzle without looking at the picture first to see what the end goal is. Now that we know what the Founding Fathers wrote, we can dig into almost two hundred fifty years of arguments about what they meant.

The First Amendment may be only forty-five words long, but it's carried much of the water for the entire nation's experiment in self-government. It tells the most powerful entity around these parts, the government itself, to keep its hands off your voice, your pen, your assembly and your petitions. That's where the story begins.

CHAPTER 2
WHAT'S COVERED IN THE FIRST AMENDMENT?

The Five Freedom Combo Meal

I f the First Amendment were lunch, it wouldn't be the "sandwich only" option. It's more like one of those supersized combo meals. Like a jumbo burger package deal, the sandwich part gets most of the glory, but the meal just isn't the complete experience without the fries, Coke and Avengers action toy.

Similarly, the First Amendment is a five-component bundle, but freedom of speech receives the most attention.

Here's the full package deal:

1. Freedom of religion
2. Freedom of speech
3. Freedom of the press
4. The right to assemble
5. The right to petition the government

They look so simple and unambiguous when you boil them down to a bullet list. However, each of these has been the center of countless courtroom dramas, sucking up thousands (millions?) of billable hours by just as many lawyers.

At first glance, these look a little bit unrelated. Why aren't they itemized separately in the Bill of Rights? As we'll see, the overlap is actually significant, kind of like how your combo meal has one consistent ingredient—grease. Well, maybe not the Coke, but the sugar makes up for that oversight.

It's unusual, if you think about it. Five enumerated freedoms the government is chartered to protect, crammed into forty-five words, and all in one Amendment. Why bundle them together? That's because the Founders understood something that's still true today: these rights are interlocking gears.

Free speech without a free press doesn't get far. What would the free press write or broadcast about? Approved topics only?

The right to assemble and protest doesn't mean much if you can't ask or demand something of the authorities. And what could you say during that protest?

Unless you believe in monitoring thoughts, religion without free speech is a shrimp cocktail without that slightly spicy sauce.

But, taken together, they're democracy's Lego set. Let's unpack them one by one.

Freedom of Religion

> *"...establishment of religion, or prohibiting the free exercise thereof..."*

The freedom of religion component of the First Amendment is neatly divided into two defining clauses. Together, they protect your right to believe whatever you want while preventing the government from controlling your spiritual life through the exercise of religion.

If you want to sound extra-informed, you can discuss these concepts as:

- The Establishment Clause: The government can't create or favor an official religion. Ever heard of "The Church of England?" That can't exist in the United States as long as the Bill of Rights is in effect.
- The Free Exercise Clause: You can choose to believe and practice (or not practice) whatever faith you choose. The government has no say in the matter.

These two very simple-sounding concepts have, and still do, cause much angst in the court of public opinion and the actual courts.

Can a town celebrate a religious holiday? Can a city construct a nativity scene? Can a public school teacher or coach pray with students or players? And to add infinite complexity, can a business refuse to serve customers if it conflicts with the business owner's religious beliefs? The Court has spent decades untangling these questions. And they're still not fully resolved.

We're going to dedicate a whole chapter to sharing some of the landmark cases, but for now, consider these two.

In the 1962 Engel v. Vitale case, New York's Board of Regents had approved an optional, non-denominational prayer to be used in schools, way back in 1951. Folks sued, claiming it violated the Establishment Clause. The Supreme Court ruled it unconstitutional. The ruling claimed that by writing the prayer, the government was establishing a religion.

In another case, Employment Division v. Smith in 1990, Alfred Smith and Galen Black were fired from their jobs as drug rehabilitation counselors after they ingested peyote, a hallucinogenic. They consumed it as part of a Native American Church ceremony. Oregon denied unemployment, citing that peyote use was illegal in the state.

The Supreme Court eventually sided with Oregon, basically saying that as long as state laws were "neutral" and didn't target a specific religion, there was no protection for religious exemption in the event of a conflict. A couple of years later, Congress passed the Religious Freedom Restoration Act to swing the pendulum back slightly in favor of religious exemptions.

The extreme example is easy. Suppose you start the Church of Punching Random Strangers in the Nose. In that case, your activity won't be protected under freedom of religion, as assault is pretty illegal everywhere, and your "religious" practice is infringing on the rights of the punchees. It's the nuanced examples that the courts and lawmakers are still struggling with.

A Freedom of Speech Preview

 *"...abridging the freedom of speech..."*

We covered the basics in Chapter 1, and we'll spend most of the book on this part of the set, so for now, just remember that "speech" is more than just talking. It includes art, protests, political campaigns, and even wearing a T-shirt with a slogan. And don't forget to include certain symbolic acts like those armbands and burning the American flag.

Think of "the talking" one plus some other forms of speech as the star player on the team. It gets most of the attention, but it performs best when all the others are in the game, too.

Freedom of the Press

"...or of the press...

Here's a question to ponder for a second. Why did the Founders single out "the press" when it's basically just written speech? We've already discussed how "speech" applies to other forms of communication.

It's because they knew that the media actually had real power to act as a check on the government. Especially back in the days before individuals had the ability to reach a large audience through modern tools like social media.

In revolutionary times, and for a century or two after, the individual had no real way to "speak to the masses" outside of the proverbial soapbox on the corner. They certainly had no efficient way to communicate directly with others farther away than walking or "horse" distance.

In that environment, the media did have the critical mass and infrastructure for broader communication through newspapers and pamphlets. That ability was a viable way to provide checks and balances on government authority. It was pamphlets, newspapers, and political essays that fueled the Revolution and ratification debates. If you could silence the press, you could control the narrative.

One of the big moments in court regarding freedom of the press was the Pentagon Papers Case, The New York Times v. United States, in 1971. The Nixon administration tried to block publication of leaked Vietnam War documents, citing national security. The Court smacked down that request, essentially saying that prior restraint (preventing publication before it happens) is almost never justified. The press's watchdog role was once again affirmed. In this case, the administration was trying to keep unfavorable news out of the public eye.

It's important to note that there have been plenty of times when the government has "leaned on" the media to keep stories out of the public eye in the interest of national security or safety. It's equally important to note that many of these occasions technically represented voluntary action by the media, as the government cannot "force" the silencing of the press except in very unusual circumstances.

For example, the D-Day landings in World War II were such large-scale operations that media outlets were bound to learn at least some of the details in advance. The government requested that they keep a lid on the secrets in the interest of national security and the safety of the U.S. troops. They did. Other World War II examples included the code-breaking operations at Bletchley Park and the Manhattan Project, which led to the development of the atomic bomb.

During the Cuban Missile Crisis, the press agreed in most cases to keep the secret of Soviet missiles in Cuba until the White House officially announced the story. Numerous similar examples have demonstrated voluntary cooperation between the government and the press, almost always for safety and national security reasons.

Today, the definition of "the press" has changed. Social media has laid the technical infrastructure for everyone with a smartphone to be a broadcast "journalist." Are they "trained" in journalism? Nope. Does it matter? The courts are still working that out, but so far, it seems protection of the "press" is being applied pretty broadly.

Right to Assemble

"...the right of the people peaceably to assemble..."

This one has been at the top of the headlines for the past decade, give or take. Of course, broad-scale protests are nothing new in the United States. We even had one, starting back in 1861, where half the country started shooting at the other half. And it wasn't the only time "public assembly" turned violent.

Historically, the right to assemble has generally been understood to include group projects (to amplify one's individual opinions and voice) like rallies, marches, and demonstrations. Classic examples include the women's suffrage parades in the early 1900s, the Civil Rights marches of the 1960s, and antiwar protests on college campuses during the Vietnam era.

But "peaceably" is the key word. Assemble to chant, sing, and wave signs? Protected. Assemble to throw rocks through windows or set things on fire? Not so much.

A big case on this one was the NAACP v. Alabama in 1958. Alabama was resisting efforts of the NAACP to operate in the state and wanted the organization to hand over its membership lists. The NAACP claimed this move would subject members to harassment and even safety concerns. The Court ruled that freedom to assemble also implied the freedom to associate privately without government intimidation. If you can't associate freely, you certainly can't assemble.

Like protests that turn violent, there are cases of assembly that come under pressure as they are not necessarily constitutionally protected. For example, occupying private property under the guise of the right to assembly generally doesn't fly.

Right to Petition the Government

"...to petition the Government for a redress of grievances..."

Here's the quiet one, often overlooked as it lives in the shadow of speech, religion and the press.

The terminology is still straightforward, but for extra clarity, "petition" in this context simply means that you have the right to formally complain to the government. Can you stand outside City Hall carrying a sign demanding they get around to fixing that pothole on your street? Yes. Can you tell everyone you know you think a president is doing a lousy job? Yes. Can you complain about the ineffectiveness of Congress to the other moms and dads at your kid's birthday party? Also, yes. You get the idea. It's OK to complain about the government. Of course, making threats is a different story, but we'll get into the exceptions later.

This seems like a no-brainer in our modern world. We've all grown up with the freedom to complain being a natural, and super-American attribute. But it's not that way everywhere (we're looking at you, North Korea and lots of others) and it hasn't been that way forever (we're looking at you, King George).

So, "petitioning the government" covers a lot more ground than a list of signatures. Of course, you can certainly do that, too, under Constitutional protection.

It's the least glamorous of the combo meal of clauses, but it closes the loop: speech lets you complain, press amplifies it, assembly shows strength in numbers, and petition makes sure the government actually hears you, whether or not they admit it.

Why Bundle These Together?

You know how, no matter how serious your sweet tooth, you can't make a cake just out of sugar? Flour provides the bulk, but on its own, makes a lousy cake. Eggs add some color, moisture, and leavening. Yeast makes it rise. Sugar provides the sweetness. You get the idea.

The various components of free speech are kinda like that. The Founders didn't cram five freedoms into one sentence by accident or to save on paragraphs. They understood that democracy doesn't run on a single liberty, much like a cake doesn't work when made from just eggs. It needs a number of complementary components. Religion keeps government out of your conscience. Speech gives individuals a voice. Press shares information. Assembly builds movements. Petition turns movements into action.

Together, they form the backbone of the American experiment. Lose one, and the others weaken. Keep all five strong, and the system stays healthy. Not necessarily comfortable or stress-free, but functional.

When people say "the First Amendment," they usually mean free speech. But the amendment is bigger, broader, and quite frankly, smarter than that. It's a small but powerful ecosystem of freedoms working together.

CHAPTER 3
THE ROAD TO THE BILL OF RIGHTS

W e take the Bill of Rights for granted these days, but we came really close to not having one at all.

The Founders almost didn't bother with a Bill of Rights. Many of them argued it was unnecessary. Why? In their mind, living in the moment of revolution and having just come out from under the thumb of governmental tyranny, many of them believed that enumerating protection of specific rights was plain and obvious for all to understand. How could anyone possibly believe a future government could trample on things like free speech or other fundamental rights?

After all, the sole purpose of government is to protect its citizens' natural rights. Under the new Constitutional model, people and states held all the power except that which was specifically itemized and delegated to the federal government, so what could go wrong without a specific Bill of Rights?

Writing down a Bill of Rights was considered redundant and even dangerous. By listing freedoms, would it be assumed that things not specifically itemized on the list were not freedoms? That's happened throughout history.

For example, if a "bill of rights" doesn't explicitly say that I have the right to paint my living room purple, could some future government claim the Department of Living Room Visual Sensibility Maintenance had jurisdiction over the matter because it wasn't itemized in the Bill of Rights?

This chapter dives into the brawl between Federalists (who didn't see a need for a Bill of Rights) and Anti-Federalists (who demanded a Bill of Rights), and how James Madison, who once doubted the need, ended up writing the most famous list of "don'ts" in history.

The Constitution Without a Bill of Rights

So, remember, the initial Constitution contained no Bill of Rights, and, therefore, no explicit free speech or freedom of religion (and all the rest) protections. It was during the ratification stage that arguments began in earnest over whether it needed one.

Alexander Hamilton wrote a few essays in his time, and during the debate over the need (or lack thereof) for a Bill of Rights, he had one ready to go, explaining why a Bill of Rights was not necessary. In Federalist No. 84, he argued that listing specific rights was dangerous:

> *"Why declare that things shall not be done which there is no power to do?"*

In other words, if the government didn't have the power to mess with your speech in the first place, why write it down? Remember, the position was this. The government started with zero power. The only "authority" it was to have was that explicitly defined in the Constitution. You can look at the list of specific "powers" the federal government has in Article I, Section 8. Nowhere in there does it say the government can limit speech or control religion. So, in Hamilton's (and the other Federalists') view at the time, a Bill of Rights was superfluous.

Worse, Hamilton warned, listing some rights might imply that any rights not listed were fair game for government abuse, especially down the road. As the system matured, human nature might begin to exert its relentless influence.

It was the ultimate lawyer's move: "If we don't say anything, then technically your rights are safe."

But many Americans weren't buying it.

Anti-Federalist Pushback

Not everyone trusted this shiny new federal government. The Anti-Federalists (you might also think of them as the skeptics of the new Constitution) worried that without explicit guarantees, the Constitution would become a blank check for tyranny, especially down the road, as people became more complacent, as they tend to do.

It's important to remember that the "downsides" of not having freedoms were very fresh in everyone's mind. In a generation or two, those running the government and the citizens alike would never have lived under oppression of any kind. The model had to work after the raw wounds of revolution had healed.

In state ratifying conventions, fiery essays and pamphlets written with pen names like "Brutus" and "Cato" warned that liberty would die a slow death if limits weren't nailed down in very clear black and white terms. "Trust us," said Hamilton and Madison. "No thanks," replied the Anti-Federalists.

In places like Virginia, Massachusetts, and New York, ratification debates got heated. Many delegates only agreed to approve the Constitution on the promise that amendments enumerating real, enforceable protections of individual liberty would follow in short order.

The Compromise for Ratification

The Constitution was officially adopted when the ninth state, New Hampshire, ratified it on June 21, 1788, but it had been done without a Bill of Rights. The new nation was still wobbling politically as ratification had been completed, for lack of a better term, under a bit of duress. States had accepted the new system, but the owners' manual of the new structure didn't yet spell out what it couldn't do. There was a clear promise to develop, document and ratify an official Bill of Rights—fast.

The pressure for amendments became impossible to ignore. It was one of the great "fine print" deals in American history: approve the Constitution now, we'll fix it later. Promise!

James Madison's Pivot

Here's the twist: James Madison, the so-called "Father of the Constitution," originally sided with Hamilton. He also thought a Bill of Rights was unnecessary. Rights, he believed, were protected by the structure of the Constitution itself.

But Madison was also a shrewd politician. He realized that public trust in the new government depended on meeting people where they were, not in some theoretical political construct. Where were they? Nervous.

Gradually, he came around to understand, and even appreciate, the benefits of a carefully constructed Bill of Rights. In 1789, as a member of the new House of Representatives, Madison introduced a package of amendments.

In a speech to Congress, he had called them "parchment barriers" against government power. He didn't think they would stop tyranny all by themselves, but he knew they mattered as a declaration of principle.

You might think of it like putting a lock on your door. Will it stop every attempt at burglary? No. But it sends a message that your home is not easy pickings.

Drafting and Approval

Madison's "change of heart" wasn't just a political maneuver to gain compromise. He came to believe in the concept, eventually becoming a key architect of the Bill of Rights. He gained inspiration from existing state constitutions, especially Virginia's Declaration of Rights, drafted by George Mason in 1776. His first draft had 17 amendments. Congress later trimmed that down to 12.

When the states voted, 10 Amendments made it through the ratification process. Those became the Bill of Rights we know today, ratified in 1791.

Fun fact: the original "First Amendment" wasn't about speech at all. Rather, it was about how big the House of Representatives should be. It failed. Another, dealing with congressional pay raises, wasn't ratified until 1992 (as the 27th Amendment).

That's how the speech/press/religion bundle wound up at the very top of the list.

So the First Amendment's #1 position? It's partly an accident of history. But it sure looks intentional now. Funny how things work out sometimes.

Early Reactions

When an argument is settled, we don't easily let go of our previous beliefs, and advocates and opponents of this debate were no different. Not everyone was impressed at first. Some Federalists grumbled that it was symbolic fluff and superfluous, bordering on dangerous. Jefferson, writing from France, loved it. Others shrugged and went back to farming.

But it helped the citizenry understand and appreciate their newly protected freedoms. But over time, the Bill of Rights became the most celebrated part of the Constitution. The promises written there became the measuring stick for every argument about liberty that followed.

In the end, that clash created something uniquely American: a short, simple, and at least seemingly unambiguous list of rights that said to government, "These are off-limits." However, as we'll see, we've managed to create a concept that seems simple, yet is difficult and challenging at times.

The Constitution gave the new government structure and power. The Bill of Rights gave it clear and easily communicated boundaries. Without the First Amendment, the United States might still have had elections, legislatures, and presidents, but it would not have had the same noisy, opinionated, argumentative, meme-loving constitutional republic we know today.

Sometimes the most important words are the ones that almost didn't make it onto the page.

CHAPTER 4
OLDER INFLUENCES ON FREE SPEECH

W hile we might have invented the Frisbee, the Ice Cream maker and the Pet Rock, America didn't invent free speech.

The Founders had seen what happened under British censorship, remembered the trial of a cheeky New York printer named John Peter Zenger, and studied the ideas of European political thinkers like John Milton and Voltaire. This chapter traces the DNA of American free expression.

The English Backdrop

We're so used to freedom of speech in practice that it's difficult to appreciate how much freedom of expression has been trampled throughout history.

For most of history, rulers treated speech like a dangerous weapon that had to be tightly controlled.

England was no exception. Criticizing the king, Parliament, or church officials could land you in prison for seditious libel. Even worse, under English law, truth was no defense. You could be punished for publishing accurate criticism, because the truth made the criticism more damaging.

Back in 1662, England even passed the Licensing of the Press Act, which required printing presses to be licensed and printed materials to be "approved." If you're a leader who is paranoid, you might think this is an effective way to keep a damper on treasonous activity. Imagine the government requiring a license for your home printer today and needing approval on the documents you create!

People got tired of this, and in 1688, King James II was overthrown during the Glorious Revolution. Soon after, the English Bill of Rights loosened the restrictions by shifting more power to Parliament over the monarchy. Things were better, but true freedom of speech remained elusive in England.

The lesson for the colonists on the American side of the ocean was clear: if they wanted real freedom, they'd need more than Britain had ever been willing to give.

John Milton's Areopagitica

Professional troublemaker, or perhaps just an agitator, John Milton (also a poet) published Areopagitica in 1644. It was a, let's say, "spunky" pamphlet arguing against pre-publication censorship. You know, that whole "we need to approve what you're about to print" thing. His argument was simple: truth and falsehood should be allowed to fight it out, publicly. The truth would ultimately win out.

Poets like Milton say it like this: "Let her (truth) and Falsehood grapple; who ever knew Truth put to the worse in a free and open encounter?"

In fairness, Milton only got close to the ideal model of free speech. He excluded Catholics, blasphemy, and a few other things from his big-tent freedom of expression ideas. But his primary point, that you don't find truth by silencing debate, was revolutionary.

The Founders had read his stuff, and the idea that free communication leads to stronger societies stuck.

Enlightenment Thinkers

Leading up to the creation of the Bill of Rights and First Amendment, the world had an arms race of sorts, with intellectuals pontificating about concepts of freedom and liberty.

First up, John Locke (1632-1704) argued that natural rights (life, liberty, property) were God-given and governments existed only to protect our rights.

A bit later, Charles-Louis de Secondat, baron de La Brède et de Montesquieu (can we agree to just call him Montesquieu?) pushed the importance of separating government powers so no one branch could smother liberty. We have at least two major examples of this theory in action: the three branches of government (Legislative, Executive and Judicial) and the composition of Congress. The unique designs of the Senate and House of Representatives are intentional and intended to "check" each other.

Voltaire (1694–1778) became legendary for his defense of the idea of tolerance of point of view and speech. He made such a big deal of it that this classic quote was falsely attributed to him: "I disapprove of what you say, but I will defend to the death your right to say it." Even if the line is apocryphal, the sentiment captures the Enlightenment-era spirit that deeply influenced the Founders.

While many modern-day citizens watch reality TV, our forefathers read and voraciously consumed this stuff.

Colonial America and the Zenger Trial

The most famous colonial free press case, because it helped kick off this whole independence crusade, along with the freedom of speech part, hit the courts in 1735. John Peter Zenger was a New York printer, and he was cranky about the royal governor, one William Cosby. So cranky, he printed critical articles about Cosby's suspected corruption and treatment of citizens in his domain.

Cosby struck back, calling two grand juries, both of which failed to find a problem. Cosby arrested Zenger anyway and charged him with seditious libel.

Big shot Philadelphia lawyer, Andrew Hamilton, stepped in and argued that truth can't be libel, even though that was not a defense under the present law. The jury agreed and set Zenger free, even though he was technically "guilty" under a ridiculous law.

The Zenger trial didn't formally change British law, but it lit a fire in the colonies. It reinforced a belief that newspapers must be free to criticize government, and that juries could push back against overzealous rulers. That spirit carried straight into the First Amendment. You go, jurors!

Religious Dissent in the Colonies

Kind of like Zenger "lived the experience" of speech critical against the government, the colonists lived the concept of freedom of religion. It wasn't some abstract, theoretical thing they discussed, but daily reality.

In fact, colonies had been founded, split, and sometimes torn apart over disputes about worship. For example:

- Roger Williams fled Puritan Massachusetts to found Rhode Island, a haven for religious liberty.
- Quakers, Baptists, and other "dissenters" faced harassment, fines, and even violence in colonies with established churches.
- A bit later, Mormons would face deadly mob violence in Missouri and Illinois.

By the time of the Revolution, Americans had lived through and seen firsthand what happens when government steps on religious beliefs. They were ready for something different.

Pamphleteering and Revolutionary Rhetoric

Back in colonial times, pamphlets were the rough equivalent of today's Twitter / X threads or long Facebook posts. Or maybe think of them like a blog post. They were cheap (easy to produce in quantity), short, and usually fiery. See? They were like social media posts! They were the primary tool to "get the word out" beyond the immediate circle of face-to-face discussions.

You've probably heard of this one. Thomas Paine's "Common Sense" sold over 100,000 copies in a matter of months. This number was astounding for the time.

Newspapers were equally influential. Local presses churned out essays, broadside point-of-view volleys, and arguments that riled up colonists and moved them toward independence.

Obviously, the British weren't keen on the relative ease of spreading this "dangerous" (to them) propaganda. Every British attempt to clamp down, like the Stamp Act that taxed printed materials, only reinforced the ideas that free speech and a free press were the oxygen of liberty.

By 1776, Americans had been practicing free speech through pamphlets and newspapers for decades, even if it wasn't legally protected, and in many cases, frowned upon.

Lessons Imported into the Constitution

When the Founders gathered to write the Constitution and Bill of Rights, they weren't starting fresh. They had lived through both censorship and open debate and had the scars to prove it:

- From England: Censorship is bad and breeds resentment.
- From Milton and Enlightenment thinkers: Truth thrives in the open discussion of ideas.
- From Zenger: A free press is essential to check power.
- From colonial religion: Free people can have diversity of beliefs, and that demands government neutrality.
- From Paine and the pamphleteers: Public debate is the high-octane fuel that powers self-government.

All of these threads were woven together into the bold experiment of the First Amendment.

If America's free speech tradition feels radical, it's because it was. In a world where kings jailed critics and churches demanded conformity, the Founders dared to declare that government must stay out of the marketplace of ideas. They didn't invent that principle out of thin air: they inherited it, adapted it, and then set it in stone. Well, parchment.

CHAPTER 5
EARLY AMERICAN FREE SPEECH BATTLES

You might think that once the ink dried on the Bill of Rights in 1791, Americans suddenly enjoyed a golden age of free expression. The reality? Not even close. Almost as soon as the First Amendment was ratified, the new government and its citizens started tripping over it. Practicing what you preach is always the hard part, isn't it?

The early republic's record on free speech is a reminder that it's one thing to declare liberty on paper, and another to live it out when politics get complicated. Once you cross from the theoretical to the real world, things can get messy.

The Ink Was Barely Dry

The First Amendment was barely out of the box before Congress tested its limits. The Bill of Rights, including number one, the free speech part, was ratified in 1791. By the late 1790s, political events started to put the theory to the test.

France and Britain were fighting, again. The new country, called the United States of America, was kind of stuck in the middle, wanting to maintain decent relations with both. One can imagine how awkward diplomatic relations were with Britain, especially given that whole War of Independence thing.

During all this chaos, President John Adams and his Federalist Party worried about foreign spies, rebellion, and domestic critics undermining the government.

The Alien and Sedition Acts (1798)

This is kind of tough to swallow and funny at the same time. The very same people who literally fought for freedom of speech (among other things of course) passed a package of laws called the Alien and Sedition Acts in 1798. One of them made it a crime to publish "false, scandalous, and malicious writing" against the government. Yes, you read that right.

Why? Who knows, but surely a major contributing factor was... fear. War with France was a distinct possibility, and the current administration was treading on thin ice. Fearing insidious activity from citizens of French ancestry and political attacks from the opposing Democratic-Republican Party, the natural response was to silence and threaten the opposition.

If that sounds like a direct violation of the First Amendment, that's because, well, it was. Federalist judges enforced the law with gusto. Dozens of Republican editors who supported Adams's rival, Thomas Jefferson, were fined or jailed. Even a member of Congress, Matthew Lyon, was locked up for criticizing Adams's "unbounded thirst for ridiculous pomp."

Jefferson and James Madison were furious. They responded with the Virginia and Kentucky Resolutions, arguing that the acts were unconstitutional. The public backlash was strong enough that when the next election rolled around, Jefferson rode the wave of outrage straight into the presidency. The Sedition Act expired in 1801.

Lesson learned: even the Founders themselves weren't immune to trampling the freedoms they'd just enshrined. But then again, we really didn't learn all the lessons, as this kind of thing popped up multiple times through U.S. history.

State-Level Struggles

As the 1800s rolled on, the fight over slavery tested the limits of free speech. In the 1830s and 1840s, abolitionists flooded the South with anti-slavery pamphlets (remember those?), newspapers, and speeches. Southern governments and mobs responded by cracking down. It's human nature, I suppose. If you aren't comfortable hearing something, just ban it.

Postmasters forgot to deliver or "lost" mail if it came in an abolitionist envelope. To cut off the "problematic" messaging, pro-slavery groups often attacked and destroyed printing facilities and presses. As one extreme example, Elijah Lovejoy, an abolitionist editor in Illinois, was murdered in 1837 while defending his printing press from a mob.

It was the classic "bad human behavior" story. Free speech sounds great and noble—on paper. But when the topic turns to something we don't like, or fear, or maybe one that exposes something unpleasant, it's something to be shut down. It's easy to support free speech when we agree with it. Not so much when it repulses us.

So, for many Americans, the idea of free speech stopped at the edge of issues they found too threatening. Abolitionists discovered that advocating for freedom could get you silenced and possibly killed.

Religious Dissent

The First Amendment protected religious freedom on paper, but old habits died hard. Remember how the text of the First Amendment reads:

> *"Congress shall make no law respecting an establishment of religion, or prohibiting the free exercise thereof..."*

In shorthand, the government shall not "establish" a particular religion. However, well into the 1800s, some states still had official churches or laws favoring certain denominations. Religious minorities representing the "not-official" faiths often paid the price.

Catholics and smaller Protestant sects suffered through these continued customs, but the most dramatic example was the Mormon experience. As the Church of Jesus Christ of Latter-day Saints grew in the 1830s and 1840s, Mormons were met with mob violence, expulsions, and even "official" hostility.

In Missouri, Governor Lilburn Boggs issued Executive Order 44, commonly known as the "Extermination Order," on October 27, 1838. It was somewhat severe in nature, in part reading, "the Mormons must be treated as enemies, and must be exterminated or driven from the State if necessary for the public peace."

If you think an edict like that might inspire violence, well, it did. Some 15,000 Mormons were driven out of the state, primarily to Illinois, where they faced more of the same, causing them to continue on to Utah. Dozens were killed in the process.

The lesson for religious dissenters was the same one abolitionists had learned: just because the right was in the Constitution didn't mean people, or even state and local governments, were eager to honor it. It was a theme that we'd see again. The law is one thing. Enforcement is another.

The Press as a Political Weapon

The First Amendment doesn't say anything about the press being partisan, and boy, if you think things are partisan now, you should have seen the action in the 1800s. In fact, I delve into this topic in more detail in my book, *The Practical Guide to America*, but a brief explanation is warranted here.

Jefferson and Hamilton, once political allies, had gravitated to a political policy war. Jefferson went so far as to get Editor Philip Freneau, of the "National Gazette," a job at the State Department so he could research spicy material to use in the National Gazette to attack Hamilton. In the opposing corner, Hamilton financially invested and provided editorial support for John Fenno's "Gazette of the United States" for the sole purpose of attacking Jefferson and his positions. Yes, true story!

And these editorial wars weren't limited to these two "frenemies." Throughout the 19th century, newspapers were fiercely partisan. Federalist, Republican, Democratic, and Whig papers all churned out scorching attacks on their opponents. These weren't the sober "just-the-facts" outlets of modern myth; they were loud, biased, and unapologetically political.

Free speech thrived in the sense that anyone could

publish. But tolerance was often a one-way street: politicians loved free speech when their side was speaking, but cried foul when the other side hurled mud back. Remember those Sedition Act laws.

The Supreme Court Stays Quiet

During this whole period, the Supreme Court sat on the sidelines of freedom of speech disputes for a number of reasons. As a result, most early speech disputes were fought out in politics (and Gazettes), not in courtrooms.

There were several reasons for this. Until the 14th Amendment in 1868, the Constitution principally applied only at the federal level. While the 14th Amendment started the incorporation process, applying constitutional principles to the states, that didn't kick into high gear until the beginning of the 20th century.

And when the courts did wade into these issues, they tended to favor the "it's OK to suppress speech when it's really important to do so" mentality. So, things like sedition, blasphemy, or political dissent were passively ruled as "OK" when the courts declined to hear cases or ruled in favor.

Not until the 20th century would the Supreme Court step in to set lasting legal standards.

That silence meant free speech lived or died on the mood of the public and the resolve of its ardent supporters. Some presses and soapboxes thrived while others were crushed under mob violence or hostile laws.

Lessons of the Early Republic

The early years of the development of practicable American free speech principles were sobering but important. They showed that the First Amendment was aspirational, and in some cases, theoretical and abstract, not automatic and certainly not rigorously enforced.

And, as the country saw time and time again, political leaders who wrote the Bill of Rights weren't always eager to obey it when the tables were turned on them and they became the target of attacks protected by the freedom of speech.

High-emotion, life and death events and issues like slavery and religion revealed how fragile real liberty can be in the face of fear and anger.

In other words, America didn't start out as a shining example of free expression. It stumbled, backslid, and contradicted itself on occasion. But those stumbles set the stage for the legal doctrines and court battles of the 20th century, when the First Amendment would finally get its teeth.

The First Amendment was born in 1791, but in its early years, it lived more like an aspiration than a reality. People fought, suffered, and sometimes died to push the country closer to the promise written on parchment. Their struggles remind us that the road to real liberty is never properly paved.

CHAPTER 6
BUILDING THE DOCTRINE: LANDMARK CASES

From "clear and present danger" in wartime (Schenck v. United States) to a kid's right to wear a black armband in school (Tinker v. Des Moines), the courts have hammered out what free speech really means. And they still are. This chapter walks through the greatest hits of Supreme Court showdowns that defined and redefined the rules of free speech.

Why Court Cases Matter

The First Amendment is famously short at just 45 words, and they look clear enough on paper. But those words didn't come with an instruction manual. And we're human, so we seem to be able to come up with all sorts of crazy permutations to make things plenty confusing.

The Founders never explained precisely what counted as "speech," how far "the press" could go, or whether schoolkids wearing protest armbands should be treated the same as politicians blathering in front of a bank of microphones.

Enter the courts. Over the years, judges have had to answer questions we've managed to create.

Could a state throw someone in jail for handing out anti-war pamphlets?

Could a high school student get suspended for wearing a jacket with four-letter words on it?

Could a protester burn the American flag?

Could corporations spend unlimited money on campaign ads?

And what about social media? That opens up a whole new can of worms. Is it the new digital town square, where everyone can speak freely? Or does it fall under the "this is a private company that can do what it likes" umbrella?

Every time one of these questions landed on the Supreme Court's docket, the justices weren't just deciding the fate of one person. They were setting the boundaries of free speech for the entire country. That's why this chapter matters. It's not a dry list of legal mumbo jumbo and rulings; it's the story of how the First Amendment grew from a simple but vague principle into a detailed doctrine that governs everything from classrooms to Facebook feeds.

Think of what follows as the highlight reel of free speech law. There's far more than I could ever cover here, or in a complete volume, filling your garage, for that matter. But each case is a snapshot of Americans arguing, pushing, and testing the limits of liberty. Taken together, they show how the First Amendment has evolved, and why today you can wear an armband, publish a tough editorial, or protest against your government.

The Incorporation Breakthrough: Gitlow v. New York

This one was a big deal for a couple of reasons.

Benjamin Gitlow was arrested and later convicted for distributing leaflets calling for strikes, socialism, and even hinting at action against the government. The specific charge? Criminal anarchy.

His defense was that the "speech" didn't present an immediate call to unlawful action, so it was allowed under the existing "clear and present danger" doctrine. He lost, appealed, and lost again.

The Supreme Court, in 1925, upheld his conviction, but using a different standard of the "bad tendency" test. Basically, that said, the state (government) could deny "speech" that has a tendency to incite dangerous action. In a way, it was the logic of a government version of self-defense. If all the elements are there, and that one is in danger, you don't have to wait until you're beaten to defend yourself.

The second big deal was that this case established the incorporation movement. This was the process of applying federal constitutional protections at the state level. The court ruled in this case that the 14th Amendment's Due Process clause applied to states as well.

> *"...nor shall any State deprive any person of life, liberty, or property, without due process of law..."*

So, in this case, the incorporation move applied constitutional freedom of speech to the states. Gitlow became a landmark case, ensuring that constitutional liberties were protected everywhere.

So the bottom line is that Gitlow lost his case... everywhere. But in the process, he, perhaps unknowingly, set a major precedent which has helped protect free speech rights for all Americans, regardless of which state they reside.

Speech in Wartime: Schenck v. United States

During World War I, Charles Schenck, general secretary of the U.S. Socialist Party, distributed leaflets urging resistance to the draft. His message was that the draft was unconstitutional and Americans should not respond to it. Obviously, this made the government unhappy, and Schenck was charged under the Espionage Act of 1917 for attempting to interfere with military recruitment.

The case made its way to the Supreme Court, with Schenck's primary argument being that he was protected under free speech principles. The Supreme Court ruled... nope!

In the ruling, Justice Oliver Wendell Holmes, Jr. introduced the "clear and present danger" test. This basically said that the government can limit free speech if that speech presents a "clear and present danger" to important government interests. This is the standard that the Gitlow case adjusted later in 1925. Holmes also clarified that speech may be more "protected" in peacetime or outside of significant government interests than during times of war.

Remember, the Schenck case is the origin of the classic line about yelling "fire" in a crowded theater. Holmes famously said, "The most stringent protection of free speech would not protect a man in falsely shouting fire in a theatre and causing a panic."

This case gave the government wide latitude to restrict speech in wartime. Later cases would narrow it, but

Holmes's phrase became one of the most misquoted lines in American law.

Expanding Dissent: Abrams v. United States

George Washington was on the right track when he made this observation during the Whiskey Rebellion era:

> *"Truth will ultimately prevail where pains is taken to bring it to light."*

In the process of losing, Justice Oliver Wendell Holmes, months after being on the winning side of the ruling in the Schenck case, wrote a dissent that just might have been more influential than the ruling itself.

In this case, Jacob Abrams and four other Russian immigrants were arrested under the terms of the Sedition Act, an amendment to the Espionage Act of 1917. The authorities claimed they were illegally producing and distributing pamphlets critical of the United States' interfering with Russia during the Bolshevik Revolution. Because the message encouraged strikes against ammunition and war material plants, the government wasn't too pleased. There was a war on after all.

The case made its way to the Supreme Court, and in a 7-2 decision, the court upheld the convictions, applying the previous logic of the "clear and present danger" test.

The two dissenting judges were Justice Oliver Wendell Holmes Jr. and Justice Louis Brandeis. They argued that unless there was an imminent threat of immediate harm, then free speech should be allowed. If you notice a refinement of Holmes' views from the Schenck case, you're right!

In the dissenting arguments, Holmes introduced the

"marketplace of ideas" logic. Basically, he claimed, "the best test of truth is the power of the thought to get itself accepted in the competition of the market."

This idea had staying power and became the critical result of the Abrams case.

See? George Washington had the right idea.

Defining the Line: Brandenburg v. Ohio

Big, precedent-setting cases can be few and far between. Almost a half-century after the Abrams decision, a new case established the "limits of free speech test" we're still using today.

Clarence Brandenburg was a Ku Klux Klan leader in Ohio who got in hot water mouthing off and inviting a TV crew to film the action. His speech at a Klan rally was plenty racist and inflammatory, but what got him in trouble with the law was the blurred line between "advocacy" and "imminent action." He was making vague statements suggesting possible actions against the government and possible retaliation, marches, and indirect threats of violence.

Brandenburg was arrested under Ohio's criminal syndicalism statute, and, you can see this coming, the case made its way to the Supreme Court.

The big court struck down Brandenburg's conviction and invalidated the Ohio law used to arrest him in the first place. In the process, the Supreme Court established a new benchmark "test."

Speech cannot be banned unless it is "directed to inciting or producing imminent lawless action" and "likely to incite or produce such action."

So, if you're keeping track, the new standard is the

"imminent lawless action" test. Speech can only be punished if it is intended and likely to produce immediate illegal acts. In practical terms, this standard limits the government's power to criminalize inflammatory speech.

Symbolic Speech: Tinker v. Des Moines

Let's dive into some of the cases that helped (legally) define what qualifies as "speech." This one addresses the idea of "expression."

In 1965, a group of students at Des Moines, Iowa, public schools decided to wear black armbands to protest the Vietnam War. As word of the planned protest got around, the school board caught wind of it and put forth a policy banning armbands. The students did it anyway and were suspended.

This didn't go over well with parents or the students, and the families sued, citing a violation of their constitutional rights.

Yep. Supreme Court time again. In a 7-2 decision, the court ruled that students "do not shed their constitutional rights to freedom of speech or expression at the school-house gate" and that schools couldn't punish students for voicing (by expression in this case) their opinion unless it "materially and substantially interfered" with school operations. As this was a silent and peaceful protest statement, the student's actions didn't meet that test.

Why it matters: Students don't lose their First Amendment rights just because they're in school. Tinker became the cornerstone of student speech protections.

Offensive Speech: Cohen v. California

Offensive speech presents a challenge, even if literally everyone besides the "speaker" agrees it's offensive.

As we get into this one, keep in mind that things were a bit different in 1968. Just think of the differences now and then of what's shown on prime-time television, and you get the idea.

With that backdrop, consider the reaction when Paul Cohen walked into a Los Angeles courthouse wearing a jacket emblazoned with the words, "F*** the Draft!" It caused a bit of a ruckus, and Cohen was arrested and sentenced to 30 days in jail for disturbing the peace with offensive conduct.

When the case made it to the Supreme Court, the conviction was reversed, but it was close—a 5-4 decision. In the majority opinion, Justice John Marshall Harlan II wrote that the state could not ban a single profane word displayed in public, unless there was some compelling reason. In this case, the state was unable to prove that Cohen's jacket choice had any real chance of causing a violent or dangerous public disturbance. Additionally, under court rules, the word was not "obscene" nor did it represent fighting words. Basically, the court ruled that "One man's vulgarity is another's lyric."

The big picture is that the First Amendment doesn't require civility. Saying or displaying something offensive on its own is not a good enough reason to tolerate government censorship.

Free Press vs. Government Secrecy: New York Times v. United States (Pentagon Papers)

Our national struggles with the Vietnam War provided plenty of material for court rulings. This one hit squarely on the free press concept.

A quick background: There was a lot of less-than-admirable behavior by a whole lot of people over a very long time surrounding the Vietnam War. The New York Times and Washington Post got their hands on documents that became known as the Pentagon Papers, a set of classified documents that revealed some ugly secrets about misrepresentation and other dirty laundry regarding the war. They started to publish this information.

President Nixon wasn't keen on that and tried to block publication, citing national security and potential harm to the country.

The lower federal courts initially sided with the President, but the case made its way to the Supreme Court.

In a 6-3 decision, the highest court allowed continued publication of the Pentagon Papers.

This case hit center mass on the whole concept of a free press. Everyone wrote separate opinions, but the outcomes were consistent. Justice Hugo Black captured the thinking along these lines: Only a "free and unrestrained press can effectively expose deception in government," and "the press was to serve the governed, not the governors."

Similar to the rulings on personal speech being OK unless it presents an immediate harm, the same idea applies to the press. Unless it's an immediate and direct national security risk (think, "Here's the combination to the nuclear weapons locker. Oh, and a guard won't be on duty between

10 and 11 PM"), then the press has no obligation to protect the government from embarrassment or exposure of a scandal.

Whistleblowers everywhere rely on this precedent. Of course, they can still get in trouble if the government can prove their actions created immediate harm.

Libel and Public Figures: New York Times v. Sullivan

It's time to get spicy. We've hit cases about the press, obscenity, sedition, and more, but let's not forget about slander, libel or maybe defamation.

Here's the short version. In 1960, the New York Times ran an ad targeted at the state of Alabama and a Montgomery city commissioner in particular, L.B. Sullivan. The ad was supportive of Dr. Martin Luther King, Jr. and criticized Alabama officials for their mistreatment of civil rights advocates.

Here's the problem. The ad contained some factual inaccuracies. Sullivan sued for libel and won a $500,000 judgment against the Times.

When the case reached the Supreme Court, the ruling was a unanimous 9-0 vote in favor of the New York Times, and the judgment was overturned.

The logic was along these lines. The government and public officials are held to a higher standard of public scrutiny, so angry and unpleasant attacks on public officials are protected, provided those statements aren't created out of pure malice. In this example, the factual errors were relatively minor, and the State of Alabama could not demonstrate that the errors were presented deliberately with knowledge of the falsehoods.

The bottom line is that the very American tradition of being able to criticize actions of public officials is protected, so long as you're not deliberately making up defamatory material to support your arguments.

Flag Burning: Texas v. Johnson

I know you were waiting for this one. The biggie: flag burning.

The year was 1984, and Ronald Reagan was President. Outside of the Republican National Convention, an activist, Gregory Johnson, burned an American flag to protest Reagan's policies.

Johnson was arrested and convicted based on a Texas law that prohibited desecration of venerated objects like the American flag.

When the case reached the Supreme Court, Johnson's conviction was overturned in a 5-4 decision.

The court viewed this incident as expressive conduct, and while offensive and unpatriotic to many, the act was protected under free speech. A notable nuance raised was that the court found the Texas law discriminatory based on the particular viewpoint. Flag burning in this instance was deemed illegal, while flag burning in a respectful manner, such as to retire a worn-out or damaged flag, was exempted under the state law.

The dissenting justices argued that the American flag held special status, but the majority stated that free speech cannot be overlooked because of hurt feelings or patriotic influence.

In fact, the courts delivered a double dose of this ruling. In 1989, Congress passed the Flag Protection Act to overcome this precedent, but the court struck it down again in the United States v. Eichman (1990) case for the same reasons.

Money as Speech: Citizens United v. FEC

Talk about putting your money where your speech is...

During the 2008 presidential election primaries, the non-profit group Citizens United wanted to promote and air a film that was critical of candidate Hilary Clinton. However, the Bipartisan Campaign Reform Act (BCRA), also known as McCain-Feingold, prevented entities like companies and unions from spending to promote elections content in speci-fied time windows prior to elections.

Citizens United sued, claiming a violation of the First Amendment. The Supreme Court 5-4 decision on this one struck down parts of the BCRA, saying that corporate enti-ties can spend whatever they want on political "speech" provided they don't coordinate directly with the candidates. The ruling essentially took the view that free speech exists, regardless of the status of the protected party. Whether it's an individual, a union or a corporate entity doesn't matter.

The ruling did uphold disclosure elements, so the spending party has to provide clear identification of where the message is coming from. All those Super PACs that fill our programming with political ads? They're a result of this decision.

There is still plenty of debate on this one. One side worries that those with "the money" have too much influ-ence over elections, while the individual voice is suppressed. On the other side, free speech is free speech, regardless of corporate status. We'll probably see some variation of this one in court again at some point.

Modern Tech: Packingham v. North Carolina

The classic image of free speech is the guy standing on a soapbox in the public square, saying, well, pretty much whatever he wants. Times have changed, and now we talk about the "new" public square: social media.

Lester Packingham is a registered sex offender in North Carolina.

In this state, it's against the law for registered sex offenders to use commercial social media that is accessible by minors.

Packingham had a good day, getting a traffic ticket dismissed, and posted about it on Facebook. He was then arrested for violating North Carolina law. He challenged the constitutionality of the law, arguing it was overly restrictive on free speech.

In this 2017 case, the Supreme Court struck down the state law, indicating that social media is the modern equivalent of the town square, and banning a whole class of people from using it was an overly restrictive infringement on their rights. As for banning them from contacting minors, that was fine. But prohibiting them from speaking at all in the new town square was a bridge too far.

Keep in mind, this case is directed at the government banning access to a publicly available social media platform. The social media company itself is not necessarily subject to the same rules.

What These Cases Add Up To

If you've made it this far through the greatest hits of the black-robed nine, you may have noticed a pattern. The First Amendment didn't just appear in its mature and fully-grown form the day it was ratified. It grew case by case, argument by argument, over more than a century of court-room battles. And there are surely plenty more to come.

It started with Gitlow, who technically lost but cracked open the door to applying free speech protections nation-wide. Then Schenck and Abrams fumbled around with how to navigate those national security issues, especially during wartime. By the time we reached Brandenburg, the Court had drawn a much sharper line: speech can only be punished if it's a call to immediate lawless action. And to think government leaders once got away with tossing people in jail for distributing pamphlets.

It's clear now, and after looking at some of these cases, why the Court often protects the speech that makes people most uncomfortable. Extreme political leaflets, black armbands, four-letter words on jackets, flag burnings, exposés of government lies, and even unlimited spending by groups you may not like are all fundamentally protected under the freedom of speech umbrella. That's the point.

The logic goes like this: if the First Amendment only protected polite, popular, widely accepted speech, it wouldn't be doing much. It would only be reflecting the views of the majority back on themselves. No one is clam-oring to censor your recipe blog or your speech praising kittens. The real test comes when speech offends, shocks, or angers. If those voices survive, then everyone's speech survives. It's all very distinctively American, isn't it?

From Zenger's colonial jury to social media tempests in teacups today, it's clear that the First Amendment bends, but remains intact. On occasion, the courts have waffled back and forth on details, but the trend is clear. The move-ment is toward more protection, not less. Free speech isn't frozen in 1791; it's alive, messy, and constantly being redefined in favor of keeping more voices in the conversation.

CHAPTER 7
WHAT FREE SPEECH DOES NOT PROTECT

Contrary to bar-stool wisdom, the First Amendment doesn't protect everything.

The First Amendment is broad, but it isn't infinite. Even the most liberty-loving judges and Founders agreed that there had to be some boundaries. Otherwise, free speech would become a shield for chaos, like threats, fraud, or outright harm.

For example, you can't threaten to burn down a house, libel your boss, or peddle hard-core obscenity and claim constitutional cover. The trick is that those boundaries are very narrow.

Over the years, the Supreme Court has carved out a handful of categories where speech can be restricted. If it doesn't fit into one of those buckets, it's almost certainly protected, no matter how unpopular or offensive it is.

Why Limits Exist

The Founders drew a line between liberty and license. Liberty meant you could speak your mind without fear of jail. License would mean you could do anything, even trample on the rights of others, under the excuse of "free speech." And, one of the fundamental underpinnings of natural rights is that you can't interfere with the rights of others. Remember the problem with a new "religion" of punching random strangers in the nose. That interferes with others' rights to life, so it doesn't fly.

That's why the Court insists that exceptions stay narrow. Better to tolerate too much speech than to give the government a blank check to censor.

From "Clear and Present Danger" to "Imminent Lawless Action"

This is the big one. If your words are intended and likely to cause immediate violence or law-breaking, they're not protected.

For example: "I call on all fellow citizens to loot the local grocery store and forcibly steal all the yummy Reese's Peanut Butter Cups. Feel free to beat up the stock guy if he gives you any trouble," would not fall under protected speech.

It wasn't always so strict. In Schenck v. United States, the Court gave us the "clear and present danger" test, which allowed the government to shut down a lot of anti-war speech during World War I. But half a century later, in Brandenburg v. Ohio, the Court drew a much tighter line: only speech intended to incite imminent lawless action can be punished.

So chanting "Someday we should overthrow the government!" is protected. Shouting "Let's storm City Hall right now!" is not.

True Threats and Intimidation

The First Amendment doesn't protect serious threats of violence. If you tell your neighbor, "I'm going to burn down your house tonight," that's not political debate or a free speech opinion. It's a crime.

In Virginia v. Black, the Court ruled that cross burning can be considered a "true threat" if it's done with the intent to intimidate. It's hard to imagine someone setting fires with a message in your front yard as anything but intimidating. Context always matters in such things. For example, burning a cross at a rally may be ugly political speech, and technically not illegal, but burning it on someone's lawn is a direct and personal threat.

Everyday examples include bomb threats, stalking, and death threats. Speech that directly puts someone in fear for their safety isn't protected.

Fighting Words

Watch the road rage, folks...

Of course, there are infinite other examples, but the underlying principle is the same. Not every insulting comment is protected by freedom of speech.

In Chaplinsky v. New Hampshire, the Court said that "fighting words," as in face-to-face insults likely to provoke an immediate fight, aren't covered by the First Amendment.

That sounds like a broad exception, but in the real world, courts almost never uphold convictions for fighting words today. Society has developed thicker skin (or maybe just more lawyers). Modern doctrine leans heavily toward protecting even harsh insults, leaving "fighting words" as more of a thing of the past than a robust rule. Maybe that has something to do with us losing the tradition of a duel at dawn?

Defamation: Libel and Slander

The right to free speech doesn't give you the right to knowingly ruin someone's reputation with lies. That's where defamation law comes into play.

To clarify things, remember "speech" can take many forms and therein lies the distinction between libel and slander. Libel refers to malicious and intentional lies using written speech, while slander refers to similar actions using verbal speech. Under both, the victim has legal recourse and can sue.

But here too, the Court has developed a narrow definition. In the New York Times v. Sullivan case in 1964, the justices ruled that public officials must prove they were the victim of "actual malice" to win a defamation case. The statement must have been made knowing it was false or with reckless disregard for the truth. That high bar, especially for public officials, ensures vigorous debate about public figures isn't stifled by endless lawsuits.

Here's a modern example that sheds light on "insults" vs. "defamation." Or, in this one, maybe it muddies the waters. You can decide.

When those kids on a Thai soccer team got stuck in a cave back in 2018, Elon Musk suggested using a mini submarine to rescue them. British cave diver Vernon Unsworth responded that Musk's idea was a "PR stunt" and that he could "stick his submarine where it hurts."

In response, Musk publicly called Unsworth "pedo guy." Apparently, according to Musk's testimony in the trial, this is a common insult in South Africa and has nothing to do with an accusation of pedophilia. Musk apologized in and outside of court during the $190 million defamation lawsuit.

The California jury agreed and quickly found no defamation, thereby helping to raise the bar for offhand insults.

So you can harshly criticize your mayor or senator. But if you knowingly spread lies about your neighbor that actually cost them their job, don't expect the First Amendment to bail you out.

Obscenity and Child Pornography

Not all expression qualifies as speech in the constitutional sense. In Miller v. California back in 1973, the Court laid down the Miller Test for obscenity. Obscene material is unprotected if it appeals to prurient interest, depicts sexual conduct in a patently offensive way, and lacks serious literary, artistic, political, or scientific value. Is that vague enough for you and chock full of judgment calls?

Here's what happened. Marvin Miller operated a mail-order business selling pornographic books and films. So far, no problem under free speech constitutional law. He got into trouble with the state of California when he started sending unsolicited mail advertisements to random addresses (people who were not his existing customers). Someone complained, and the state successfully prosecuted Miller under its obscenity law.

Miller appealed, and when the case made it to the Supreme Court, he lost again under a 5-4 ruling. In the ruling, the court established those three tests: prurient interest (excessive or unhealthy interest in sexual matters), patently offensive and lacking artistic merit.

Adult pornography is generally protected unless it

crosses the "Miller line." That's why courts distinguish between explicit but lawful material and obscene works deemed valueless. The boundary is messy, but the principle is firm: obscenity and exploitation don't get First Amendment shelter.

There is one absolute in this. Child pornography is never protected under constitutional free speech, period.

Commercial Speech (with Limits)

When you're paying to deliver a message, the courts have established a higher standard for constitutional free speech protection.

Advertising gets protection, but not as much as political speech. False advertising, fraud, or misleading claims can be banned outright. Note the underlying theme of "truth required" here, too.

That's why the government can crack down on cigarette ads, miracle diet pills, or snake oil "cures." Selling a product with lies is commerce, not liberty, and therefore false messages in that context are not protected.

Speech in Special Contexts

Some environments come with their own set of rules; you might think of them as practical adaptations. For example, the courts have recognized that a school, a military base, or a prison can't function like a street corner soapbox.

Students don't shed their rights at the school's front door. Remember the Tinker case regarding black armbands? The Court sided with students, ruling that symbolic protest is protected as long as it doesn't cause a "substantial disruption."

But the justices also made clear that schools aren't free-for-alls. In Bethel v. Fraser in 1986, a student's sexually suggestive speech at a school assembly got him suspended, and the Court said that was just fine. Schools can promote civility and limit vulgar or lewd expression. Later, in Morse v. Frederick in 2007, during the "Bong Hits 4 Jesus" case, the Court upheld a principal's right to discipline a student for displaying a pro-drug banner at a school event.

So yes, students have free speech rights, but they're balanced against the school's job to teach and maintain order.

In the armed forces, free speech is subservient to the command structure. A military that runs on open mic night isn't a military for long, or at least not an effective one. Service members can't publicly insult their superiors or advocate disobedience without consequences.

The Supreme Court has consistently held that military discipline and readiness outweigh rights to free speech. To be clear, soldiers can still petition Congress or express opinions privately, but when they put on the uniform, the chain of command comes first.

Inmates don't lose all constitutional rights behind bars, but those rights shrink considerably. The Court has ruled that prison officials can restrict speech, mail, and publications when needed for security, order, or rehabilitation.

The prison test is one of "reasonable relation." If a restriction is reasonably related to legitimate penological interests, it usually stands. For example, prisons can block materials that might incite violence or coordinate escape attempts. Sorry, no pamphlets saying, "OK, guys, I found a weak spot in the fence. Here's how we escape tonight!"

It's not supposed to be about silencing prisoners but rather keeping facilities safe and manageable. Still, courts have sometimes stepped in when restrictions go too far, such as banning all reading material or cutting off access to legal communication.

In each of these settings, the First Amendment still applies. It's just tuned to the environment, and the line is drawn a bit differently. The key is proportionality: restrictions must serve a real purpose, not convenience. A school can maintain discipline, but not silence political expression. The military can demand obedience, but not ideological conformity. A prison can ensure safety, but not erase a person's voice entirely.

In these cases, think of the First Amendment "flexing" rather than "breaking."

The "Fire in a Crowded Theater" Myth

If you've ever heard someone say, "You can't shout fire in a crowded theater," congratulations! In related news, if you haven't heard this, just log onto Facebook for a minute and find any political argument. I'll wait. Got it? Now, you've heard one of the most overused and misunderstood lines in American law.

The line comes from Justice Holmes in Schenck v. United States, where he said the First Amendment wouldn't protect someone "falsely shouting fire in a theatre and causing a panic." The phrase became a kind of free-speech disclaimer.

But here's the catch: that standard was abandoned decades ago. Since Brandenburg in 1969, the test has been deemed an "imminent lawless action." Shouting "fire" in a theater might get you sued if people are injured, but it's not the official rule for limiting speech.

In short, don't use this one in Facebook arguments

anymore. Someone really up to speed on free speech case law will call you out for the inaccuracy.

Why Exceptions Stay Narrow

The Court's approach to limits on speech is cautious by design. Once the government gets broad power to censor, it's hard to stop. No! Say it isn't so! The government getting an inch and taking a mile? That couldn't possibly happen. But just in case...

Today's "dangerous" speech could be tomorrow's truth. That's why exceptions are almost always defined very carefully and narrowly, not in broad sweeps.

The guiding principle is simple: the First Amendment protects everything except a few narrowly defined categories, including incitement, threats, defamation, obscenity, and fraud. If speech doesn't fit into one of those boxes, it's almost certainly protected.

Reader Checklist

Back in the introduction, I promised not to hand out cheat sheets telling you what I personally think should count as "free speech." That's not my job, and honestly, it wouldn't be very useful, and you shouldn't care about my opinion anyway. The whole point of this book is to give you the tools and the case law highlights that have shaped current definitions, so you can evaluate headlines, social media debates, and late-night arguments without relying on pundits or self-proclaimed experts.

That said, it's easy to get lost in the weeds of cases, doctrines, and exceptions. So here's a simple checklist: a quick "is this protected?" filter you can run through when you encounter a free speech controversy:

- Is it incitement to imminent violence? If the words are aimed at sparking a riot right now (think Brandenburg v. Ohio), that's not protected.
- Is it a true threat? Death threats, bomb scares, or cross burnings on someone's lawn cross the line into intimidation, not expression.
- Is it defamation, obscenity, or fraud? Lying about your neighbor in print, selling snake oil cures, or producing hardcore illegal material? Don't expect the First Amendment to back you up.

If not, odds are it's protected. And yes, that means even the speech you find offensive, shocking, or flat-out creepy is usually covered. That's the price of living in a system that values liberty over comfort. Or, you might think of it as a payoff of liberty.

The Court has set aside a handful of narrow categories where speech can be restricted, but outside those, the presumption is freedom.

The beauty of the First Amendment is that it doesn't ask whether a message is tasteful, respectful, or popular. This makes it hard to accept sometimes. It simply asks: Is it legally within those narrow exceptions? If not, the answer is almost always yes; it's protected speech.

Contrary to barstool wisdom, free speech isn't absolute. But the exceptions are rare, precise, and carefully guarded. That's what makes the First Amendment remarkable: it assumes more speech is better than less, and that bad ideas are best defeated in open debate, not in courtrooms or jails.

CHAPTER 8
THE PRIVATE VS. PUBLIC DIVIDE

I s "cancel culture" a free speech crisis or simply people exercising their right to free speech? And what happens when Facebook blocks what you want to say?

Let's untangle the complex relationship between government censorship and private consequences, illustrating why the First Amendment restrains Washington, not your social media provider or employer. Here's a preview hint: Constitutional free speech doesn't imply "no consequences ever."

If there's one First Amendment mix-up that causes near-daily angst in news stories, social media debates, and barstool arguments, it's this: the difference between government censorship and private consequences.

People often shout "free speech!" when their boss fires them, their favorite celebrity gets "canceled," or a social media company boots someone off the platform. But here's the deal: the First Amendment restrains the government, not your employer, private companies or your neighbors.

If Congress or City Hall tries to silence you, that's unconstitutional. If your neighborhood book club doesn't invite you back after your two-hour monologue about the need for an interplanetary Congress, that's just social consequences.

Who the First Amendment Applies To

The text is crystal clear on this distinction: "Congress shall make no law..."

Yes, that refers to the federal government, but starting with the passage of the 14th Amendment, that concept has been pushed to state and local governments, too. It might be easier to think of the First Amendment starting with "Government shall make no law..."

This is why your city council can't ban yard signs criticizing its policies, and your governor can't shut down rallies just because they're annoying or even calling out his or her lousy policies.

But the freedom of speech protection stops there. The First Amendment does not apply to your employer, your church, your softball league, your Homeowners Association or your social media platform. While this is nowhere in the Constitution, this line is a good one to remember: "The First Amendment protects you from Uncle Sam, not Uncle Facebook."

The Workplace Example

Let's start with our jobs.

If you work for the government, your speech rights are protected, but limited if your words interfere with the agency's function. You might think of this scenario as a bit like the military circumstance we discussed earlier. If you're a private employee, it's a whole different ballgame. *Your employer can discipline or fire you for speech that violates company policy.*

Consider teachers and professors dismissed for controversial Facebook posts or athletes disciplined for remarks that caused PR headaches to the team or athletic association.

It's important to remove the emotion from the analysis and remember that the First Amendment doesn't apply because the government wasn't the one silencing them. Free speech law may not save your job, but it does stop the local police from arresting you for the same remarks.

Here's the practical takeaway. Freedom of speech doesn't equate to freedom from consequences. The First Amendment protects you from jail, not from HR.

Social Media and Platforms

I mentioned emotion in the previous section, but perhaps I should have saved that line for this section. Social media is an emotion electromagnet. And right here is where things get even thornier. Platforms like Twitter/X, Facebook, and YouTube feel like public spaces, but legally, they're still private companies. They can boot users, flag posts, and set their own rules without violating the free speech clauses of the Constitution.

The courts have even weighed in. In Packingham v. North Carolina in 2017, the Supreme Court called social media "the modern public square." But that ruling was about government restrictions, not private moderation. Platforms may act like digital public spaces, but they're owned and operated by corporations with their own terms of service. So it's more like a private backyard than a public park.

Here's where the exception lies. While social media companies can set their own content policies, they cannot do so under instruction or pressure from the government. If the White House is leaning on said companies to ban and block people from talking about a President's obsession with Pokémon, then that activity is illegal under the First Amendment. If federal agencies lean on companies to suppress certain content, courts may decide that crosses into unconstitutional state action. Those cases are still unfolding in the digital age.

If you want more detail on the evolving statutes, consider Section 230 of the Communications Decency Act. This established immunity for social media companies from content posted by their users. It also reinforces their ability to moderate content per their established policies. There are exceptions for federal criminal law, intellectual property law and sex trafficking law.

Cancel Culture or Free Speech in Action?

Ooh boy. Let's not forget society's newest rage bait: cancel culture.

When a celebrity loses a sponsorship, a comedian's gigs dry up, or a company gets boycotted, critics call it censorship. But more often, it's counter-speech. We're right back to that "free speech doesn't mean no consequences" concept.

Just because the celebrity, comedian or company exercises their free speech, it doesn't mean they get the last word. That celebrity's audience or the company's customers may very well decide to speak out on their own. And they can. If they speak out by telling people not to tune in, buy tickets, or stop buying some company's product, there's nothing unconstitutional about that. They're just exercising their right to freedom of speech. Voting with your time, attention, or wallet is perfectly within your rights, as is using speech or social media posts to encourage others to do the same.

There's a big difference between government force and social backlash. The First Amendment guarantees you the right to speak. It doesn't guarantee you an audience, applause, or immunity from criticism. Nor does it guarantee you a continued stream of customers buying your product.

That said, social shaming and mob boycotts sure can feel a lot like censorship in practice. If everyone's terrified of losing their job or reputation for speaking honestly, free expression suffers even without government involvement. The First Amendment can't fix that; it's a cultural challenge.

Public Spaces vs. Private Property

As with nearly everything, there can be nuances with free speech. Consider the location, for example.

Free speech rights are the strongest in what the courts call traditional public forums: streets, sidewalks, parks, and the proverbial town square. These are the classic places for rallies, marches, and "soapbox" speeches. Has anyone actually seen a soapbox in the past 100 years? But I digress...

In these public spaces, the government can regulate the time, place, and manner (no bullhorns at 3 a.m. in residential areas), but not the content of your message. Rally or protest permits and such are just a part of doing business.

We've ceded authority to the government to equitably manage public spaces. Just because you have a right to free speech doesn't mean you have exclusive control over that space. It's the government's job to make sure it's equally accessible to all. So, to exercise your free speech in that public space, you might have to wait your turn.

But move onto private property, like a shopping mall, a sports stadium, or a workplace, and the rules change. The owners of private property can set speech policies, even if the space seems to be public in nature.

Here's a weird case to illustrate the significance of location. In fact, it just might be the most milquetoast ruling in this book. Or at least it seems wishy-washy.

A group of students set up a table in the food court of a California Mall to collect petition signatures opposing a United Nations action. Mall management asked them to leave. The student group complained, saying they had a right to operate in this "public space."

The local court ruled in favor of the mall, which said it was their property and their right to free speech was being violated. But the California Supreme Court and later the Supreme Court of the United States overturned that ruling. As it turns out, the California state constitution enumerates an affirmative right to free speech, and part of that is the right to free speech in publicly accessible areas of private properties, like a mall food court.

So, the Supreme Court stated that it's OK for states to expand free speech rights as long as they don't violate constitutional free speech rights at the federal level. In this case, they ruled the students did have the right to collect their petitions on private property. However, the court did make it clear that the First Amendment does not require the action.

Part of the reason for the mixed ruling was that California's constitution defined an affirmative right to free speech (citizens *can* exercise free speech in these types of scenarios…), while the federal constitution enumerates a negative right scenario, meaning the government *can't* restrict free speech.

To be clear, unless your state constitution says otherwise, you don't have a constitutional right to free speech in the food court.

Non-Governmental Censorship and Social Pressure

Following on to the privately owned spaces discussion, the First Amendment doesn't stop private censorship. For example, publishers can refuse to print certain books, social media platforms can remove posts or ban users, and TV networks can cancel a show. These aren't constitutional violations, even if they feel like censorship.

Where things get muddy is when powerful private individuals and companies control the means of communication. The lines between free speech in theory and free speech in practice get blurry.

Suppose three giant social media platforms dominate online conversation and all three ban the same viewpoints. In that case, people may rightly wonder: Do we really have free speech if the practical avenues for it are closed off? Isn't social media the modern times equivalent of the public square, even though it's privately owned?

It's a hard question. These types of activities are legal under the Constitution, but culturally, their effects can still give the impression that free speech is curtailed.

Why the Distinction Matters

Understanding the distinction between private and public is crucial. It keeps us from crying "That's a First Amendment violation!" every time a celebrity gets de-platformed or an employee loses their job. Understanding the difference also helps keep the focus on where the real dangers lie: government censorship.

The Constitution is there to keep the state from silencing citizens. Beyond that, we're left to navigate the rough waters of social pressure, company policies, and digital moderation on our own. Those can feel unfair, frustrating, or hypocritical, but they're not unconstitutional.

The First Amendment doesn't guarantee you'll be popular, immune to consequences, or endlessly platformed. And if you're mouthy, it certainly doesn't guarantee your continued employment. However, it does guarantee that the government can't shut you up. Everything else, including social media bans, workplace discipline, or angry mobs of critics, is part of the messy reality of living in a society where everyone else has free speech, too.

In other words, you have the right to speak your mind. Everyone else has the right to roll their eyes, clap back, or show you the door. That's liberty in action.

CHAPTER 9
FREE SPEECH IN WARTIME AND CRISIS

History proves that fear is the enemy of unrestricted and free expression. During wars and other times of national distress, presidents and Congress have often cracked down hard on freedom of speech. Sometimes there have been understandable reasons related to survival, but in other cases, simple paranoia is at fault.

History shows a clear pattern: in moments of crisis, Americans often trade liberty for security, only to regret it once the storm passes.

Let's explore scenarios from Lincoln's wartime measures to McCarthy's witch hunts and the post-9/11 Patriot Act to understand how crisis pressures freedom like nothing else.

Fear vs. Freedom

When people are scared, they want reassurance, not public debate or a bunch of arguments over a looming catastrophe. Government leaders know this. It's part of their job to keep the populace from freaking out. From the Civil War to COVID-19, fear has tempted governments to tighten speech controls in the name of unity or survival. As one justice observed, "When the cannons roar, the censors get busy."

Lincoln and the Civil War

Talk about extenuating circumstances to set aside constitutional protections. During the Civil War, Abraham Lincoln faced the unenviable management challenge of the country being at war with itself.

In an effort to keep some semblance of control, he suspended habeas corpus and tolerated military arrests of editors and critics who opposed the war. Some newspapers were shut down, and dissenters were jailed without trial.

The right call? Or is tossing fundamental constitutional protections out with the trash inexcusable in any circumstance? You make the call on that one.

Whatever the right answer, Lincoln justified these actions with a famous question: "Are all the laws but one to go unexecuted, and the government itself go to pieces?"

In other words, using his logic, the ends justified the means. If adhering to one law meant the downfall of the country, then that one law must be broken by Lincoln's logic.

Most historians give Lincoln credit for holding the Union together, but his actions remain one of the earliest examples of free speech sacrificed in crisis.

World War I and the Sedition Acts

Fast forward to 1917. As the U.S. entered World War I, Congress passed the Espionage Act and the Sedition Act. These laws made it illegal to interfere with the draft or criticize the government. The thinking was that the country is at war, and we need to put a stop to activity that might undermine the war effort. While the fighting was overseas, there were potential threats from an offered alliance between Mexico and Germany, so in some sense, potential survival, or at least possible harm within our borders, was on the table.

Under this new law, Socialist leader Eugene V. Debs gave a speech against the war and ended up in prison. Other volunteers handing out anti-draft leaflets were jailed, leading to the famous Schenck v. United States case.

The Court upheld these convictions, giving us Justice Holmes's "clear and present danger" test. At the time, dissenters were painted as traitors. Years later, most Americans looked back and admitted some degree of overreaction. Fear makes us do illogical things.

World War II and Beyond

World War II brought new forms of censorship. Military mail was monitored, and favorable war propaganda was carefully managed. Even Hollywood was drafted into the cause, producing war films that doubled as morale boosters.

As for military mail censorship, most didn't perceive that as some gross overstep of First Amendment rights. Remember the concept of "command priority" we discussed earlier. Besides, you couldn't risk leaks of sensitive tactical information, even if innocent in intent. "Mom! Guess what? I get to ride on this brand new aircraft carrier. We'll be departing San Diego on August 3rd at 10:30 AM!"

The darkest chapter was the internment of Japanese Americans. While technically not a speech issue, it showed how quickly civil liberties can collapse in the face of wartime fear. Voices objecting to internment were largely drowned out until decades later, when the government formally apologized and even sent restitution payments to survivors in the 1980s.

The Red Scare and McCarthy Era

After WWII, the country unlocked a whole new level of fears with the Red Threat. The potential enemy shifted from fascism to communism. The late 1940s and 1950s saw loyalty oaths, blacklists, duck and cover drills in schools in case of nuclear war, and congressional hearings grilling citizens about their political beliefs. It seemed as if everyone was accusing everyone else of being a communist or at least a communist sympathizer.

Hollywood writers and actors were blacklisted for refusing to "name names" of "fellow sympathizers." Careers were destroyed not for violence, but for opinions. Hundreds of writers, actors, directors and producers were blacklisted. Senator Joseph McCarthy turned anti-communist fervor into a crusade that chilled expression nationwide. At least until he was finally discredited. All that "evidence" he claimed to have about communist operatives infiltrating American society never materialized.

And the courts eventually pushed back, striking down loyalty oaths and protecting political association. But for a decade, just the fears of communism silenced millions of Americans.

Supreme Court Justice William O. Douglas was one of the Court's staunchest defenders of the First Amendment and freedom of speech. He famously stated that suppression "chills freedom at its core." Just the threat of censorship or government repression discourages individuals and organizations from freely expressing themselves, essentially creating a form of "self-censorship."

Vietnam War Protests

The 1960s flipped the script. While earlier events had, in fact, stifled free expression, this time, dissent refused to be silenced. Students marched and burned draft cards. Musicians wrote and performed anti-war music publicly. The town square soapbox was a busy place.

Remember the Tinker v. Des Moines case in 1969, where students won their case demanding the right to protest in school by wearing armbands.

But on the flip side, in the United States v. O'Brien case in 1968, the courts ruled that burning draft cards was not protected expression, because it interfered logistically with the draft system. That was interpreted to fall into the "clear imminent threat" to national security category.

Vietnam showed how courts were learning to draw finer lines: political expression was protected, but speech that directly obstructed government functions could be restricted.

Post-9/11 and the War on Terror

While, with one exception being the attack on Pearl Harbor in World War II, America's wars usually didn't threaten the homeland directly, September 11, 2001, was an attack that hit right at home. And the shock reshaped American attitudes overnight.

The fear element and the rush to trade liberty for security influenced free speech principles in a very big way.

The Patriot Act expanded government surveillance powers exponentially, and as later exposés (think the Edward Snowden case) demonstrated, at least some in the government expanded surveillance well past the bounds established by law. Additionally, critics of the wars in Iraq and Afghanistan sometimes found themselves publicly branded as "unpatriotic."

Civil liberties groups worried about chilled speech, secret watchlists, and a culture of suspicion. Even librarians staged protests against the incursions with "read-ins" inviting the FBI to "watch us read these questionable books."

The Supreme Court was more cautious than in past wars, but the atmosphere showed once again how a crisis shifts the balance toward security.

Pandemic-era Speech Battles

In 2020, the COVID-19 pandemic sparked a whole new kind of crisis: the fear of health misinformation. Social media platforms banned posts that spread information about cures, treatments and vaccines. Government officials pressured companies to crack down on what they perceived as dangerous content.

The legal debate here is a new take on the topic of freedom of speech: when does moderation cross into government censorship? When does trying to protect public health justify limiting expression? Who decides what discussion is or is not a threat to public health? Are social media company employees really qualified to make those decisions? The questions were, and continue to be, endless.

Courts are only beginning to sort this out, but it's clear the First Amendment is being tested in real time.

The Pattern Across History

Look back and you'll see the rhythm:

1. Something bad happens, and people get scared.
2. Government leaders tighten restrictions on free speech.
3. Courts often uphold those restrictions using logic like "imminent threats."
4. After the fact, we regret the overreach and realized we acted out of fear.

Whether it was the Sedition Acts of 1798, the jailing of World War I dissenters, the Red Scare, or pandemic-era moderation, the pattern repeats. Liberty is most at risk when people are scared.

The hard lesson of history is that speech restrictions may feel necessary in the moment, but they rarely age well. If anything, they remind us that the First Amendment's job isn't to protect easy conversations; it's to shield the messy, inconvenient, uncomfortable ones, especially when the stakes are high.

CHAPTER 10
FREE SPEECH AND NEW FRONTIERS

When the Founders wrote the First Amendment in 1791, the most advanced communication tech was a hand-cranked printing press. Today, billions of people carry smartphones that can broadcast their thoughts to the entire planet in seconds. The stage has gotten bigger, the megaphones louder, and the audience angrier.

So, social media has created a global megaphone and a massive headache. Algorithms encourage and boost outrage, deepfakes blur truth (remember when a picture or video was absolute truth), and foreign actors use bots to try to stir the pot, just because they can.

Let's consider how the First Amendment collides with twenty-first-century tech, and what lessons America can learn from other countries' approaches to speech regulation.

The Digital Megaphone

For most of the country's history, news and content were limited to those who had the means and infrastructure to share them. Newspapers, magazines, and later radio and TV stations maintained a monopoly on being able to broadly communicate information.

Now, the internet, combined with social media, has turned each of us into a publisher. What once took a printing press, ink, and a delivery system now takes only a few taps on your personal phone. With this capability, the scale of information dissemination exploded through the top of the charts. Millions of posts and articles fly by every minute, far beyond the ability of courts, governments, or even the platforms themselves to monitor in real time.

The upside? Voices that once had no platform now at least have the possibility to get heard. The downside? False information, conspiracy theories, and outright harassment can spread just as easily as truth.

And therein lies the challenge. While all have the technical capability to spread information to nearly everyone on planet earth, we can't control who will actually see what we share. Algorithms, and to some degree, our own promotion and marketing, determine how large our respective audiences are. With social media companies laser-focused on developing algorithms that maximize clicks and views, while encouraging us to remain online for as long as possible, those overlords have, in a sense, become the new Media Moguls.

Should they be in control of the dissemination of speech? Or is it their right to promote and demote to support their business models?

Social Media as the "Modern Public Square"

In Packingham v. North Carolina back in 2017, the Supreme Court struck down a law that barred registered sex offenders from participating on social media at all. Justice Anthony Kennedy called social media "the modern public square," a place where people connect, debate, and access information.

That sounds like a ringing endorsement of online expression, but here's the catch: Packingham was about government restrictions. It didn't say private platforms like Twitter/X or Facebook must allow everyone to speak. Legally, they can still set their own rules.

This leaves us with a weird hybrid: social media feels public, functions like a public space, but it is owned by private corporations with their own moderation policies.

That gray zone is where many of today's loudest debates reside. Is it the new public square? Should social media companies be treated more like the phone companies of old, where Ma Bell couldn't decide what one could or could not talk about over the phone lines?

Corporate Power vs. Government Power

The First Amendment restrains government, but what happens when most of our conversation happens on platforms run by a handful of private companies? Facebook, YouTube, and TikTok can shape what billions of people see, and their decisions aren't bound by the Constitution. Their decisions and policies are driven (presumably) by the market—their customers.

This raises the unsettling possibility that while the government can't silence you, a handful of corporations effectively can. Some argue that when a platform becomes essential for public discourse, it should be treated like a utility that's required to carry all voices. The phone companies of yesteryear and the electric company are required to serve you as long as you pay the bills, regardless of your political views and how you do or don't share your opinions. Others counter that forcing platforms to host all speech would itself be a form of government interference.

It's a constitutional tug-of-war with no clear resolution in sight. Where do you stand?

AI, Bots, and Deepfakes

The jury is out as to whether artificial intelligence will become our overlords in the process of taking over the world, but what is clear is the present impact it has on the never-ending freedom of speech discussion.

If social media wasn't complicated enough, now we've got to deal with the text, images, and even video being produced by AI at a scale no group of a million humans could match. Bots flood comment sections, fake accounts amplify outrage, and deepfakes blur the line between reality and fabrication.

AI agents are even capable of automatically answering and responding to your email, and companies are proud of this. Soon, we'll have AI bots creating emails to send to another AI bot, which answers them. Will humans ever even see any of it?

Legally, this raises strange new questions.

If AI generates speech, is that speech protected?

Who's responsible if a bot spreads lies that ruin someone's reputation?

And how do you safeguard elections when a convincing deepfake can hit the internet hours before polls open?

Courts haven't answered these yet, but the First Amendment will have to stretch into uncharted territory.

Global Comparisons

One way to appreciate America's unusual approach to speech is to look overseas. Some European countries are taking definitive action, but is that the right move?

- Germany bans Nazi symbols and Holocaust denial outright.
- The U.K. and Canada criminalize certain kinds of "hate propaganda."
- The European Union's Digital Services Act requires platforms to police harmful content more aggressively.

The big problem is this. Who defines what is hate speech? With all the accusations flying around today of nearly everything being "hate speech" to someone, it's rapidly becoming a meaningless term.

If person A accuses person B of "hate speech" for calling the sky "azure" instead of "blue," is it really? That's a silly example, but far too many of the real examples we see today are equally meaningless.

Let's very delicately wade into a real-world example that we've all seen in recent news and social media.

Team Orange says life begins in the womb. Team Yellow might call that hate speech.

Team Yellow believes life doesn't begin until birth. Team Orange believes that to be hate speech.

Who's right? Which example is "hate speech?" Neither of them? Both of them? You get the idea.

This is the fundamental reason why offensive, but nonviolent speech, is allowed in the United States.

Only one person has the authority to define what is "offensive." That's the listener.

The one toward whom the "speech" was directed. They can feel offended. Or not feel offended. Should society bow to that kind of personal and completely subjective whim? This is the key to understanding why it's impossible to broadly define "offensive" speech.

In the United States, the First Amendment would block most of those restrictions established in Europe and Canada. Our courts are far more reluctant to outlaw offensive but nonviolent speech. That makes America an outlier among democracies. It's more permissive, and sometimes more chaotic, but more protective of extreme or unpopular voices.

Speech in the Age of Misinformation

False information has always existed, but the internet straps a jetpack on it, enabling it to spread like wildfires could never dream of. Studies show lies spread faster online than facts, and that makes sense when you think about it.

A lie, by nature, is juicy and social media is nothing if not a tempting way to be the first to share spicy tidbits. Speed and the human desire to be seen as "the first in the know" overcome the sensible approach of fact-checking before sharing.

Whether it's election conspiracies, fake medical cures, or viral hoaxes, misinformation challenges the old assumption that truth always beats falsehood in the "marketplace of ideas." New policies like community notes-type solutions seem to help—some. But again, the lie spreads far faster than the correction. And in a highly charged political environment, we humans tend to want to "fact-check" opinions more than actual facts.

Should the government step in to regulate misinformation? The danger, of course, is that once the government starts deciding what's true and false, the door to censorship opens wide. Pick your political aisle. Now ponder how much you trust the opposite side to define true from false. Yeah, I know, that's absurd!

The Founders bet that open debate was the best defense against bad ideas. Whether that bet still holds in the age of clickbait and bots is one of the defining free speech questions of our time.

The Future of Free Speech

I bet you're starting to look in the crystal ball and seeing a hazy outlook for freedom of speech discussions...

We've got all sorts of looming questions for our courts to address:

- Should AI-generated content be considered "speech"?
- Should platforms be treated as public utilities or remain private fiefdoms?
- Should libel and defamation laws be updated for the digital age, where reputations can be destroyed in minutes?

No one knows how these questions will play out. What's clear is that the First Amendment isn't a relic; it's a living rulebook being tested daily.

That's the beauty of principles that were defined in the Bill of Rights. It doesn't even try to define all the details in advance, but rather establishes a principle: *free people should have the right to speak their mind and express themselves.* The government should never intrude on that right. The details on how to apply that principle are up to us as the times change.

The First Amendment has weathered wars, sedition laws, and cultural revolutions. Now it faces the wild frontier of technology, where memes can topple reputations, bots can sway elections, and AI can imitate anyone's voice.

The challenge is the same as it's always been: balancing liberty with order, truth with danger, democracy with chaos. Free speech has never been easy. And if history is any guide, the First Amendment will stretch, wobble, and adapt, because silencing voices has always proven more dangerous than letting them be heard.

CHAPTER 11
WHY IT ALL STILL MATTERS

Free speech isn't just words on 200+-year-old parchment. It's the beating heart of democracy. Without it, corruption festers, ideas stagnate, and citizens (especially those in the minority court of public opinion) lose their power to push back. Now, let's pull everything together, showing how the "marketplace of ideas" works, and giving you a simple framework for judging whether today's controversies fall inside or outside of the First Amendment.

The Marketplace of Ideas

During the Abrams v. United States case in 1919, Justice Oliver Wendell Holmes gave us the "marketplace of ideas" support for the value of free expression of speech and ideas. His point was that the best test of truth isn't whether government approves of it, but whether its logic survives in open debate.

The marketplace metaphor isn't perfect because we

humans somehow manage to screw most anything up. Consider the scenario where false ideas sometimes go viral while truth never really catches up. But I'd argue the alternative is far worse. Once the government becomes the referee of what's "true" or "acceptable," debate withers and power goes unchecked. Worse, "truth" changes meaning depending on who's in charge at the moment.

Imagine referees deciding which team is allowed to score before the game even starts. That would be like pro wrestling! Sorry, just kidding. That's what censorship does. The First Amendment insists that every team takes the field, and the crowd decides who wins based on measurable performance.

Free Speech as a Safety Valve

If you think about it, free speech is a little bit like our election system. In many countries throughout history, someone attains power and stays there until someone more sneaky, or maybe more powerful, kicks them out. However, in the United States, we have free elections that allow people to express their opinion on leaders' performance every two, four or six years. With this "pressure valve," there's no need for repeated American Revolutions. We let off steam with every election, peacefully. Not without angry words, but usually without a war.

Similarly, you might think of free speech like a pressure valve on a boiler. Without it, frustrations and grievances build up until they explode. Allow people to protest, complain, and argue out loud, and the system releases pressure before it blows apart. Sure, it can get ugly, but words are a lot better than bullets.

History proves this point. Civil Rights leaders, women's suffragists, and abolitionists all used speech, assembly, and petition to channel anger into reform. In Montgomery, Alabama, it was anger that drove thousands of citizens to boycott the bus system until segregation was ended for public transportation. Silencing people would have driven their movements underground, where the anger might have turned violent.

Allowing speech doesn't guarantee peace, but banning it almost always guarantees unrest.

Protecting the Unpopular

There's another analogy between free speech and the American system. The United States isn't a democracy, although it is run by democratic principles. A democracy only protects the rights of the majority. That's 51%, or perhaps less if we're choosing between more than two options. The American system is a Constitutional Republic, designed precisely to consider the will of the majority, but still protect the rights of the minority.

Similarly, free speech principles protect the minority, whether it be opinions, voicing political beliefs, defining art, or an infinite number of other forms of expression. The Court has repeated this lesson again and again: the First Amendment isn't there to protect polite dinner conversation. It's there to protect the speech people hate. If you understand the reasoning behind those two extremes, all the stuff in the middle makes a lot more sense.

Abolitionists, suffragists, anti-war protesters, and civil rights activists were almost always unpopular—at first. But over time, many of them made America better in some way.

If the government had been free to shut them up, progress would have been suffocated.

This is precisely why some of the cases we've discussed, like Cohen v. California ("F*** the Draft") and Texas v. Johnson (flag burning), are so important. They weren't about polite slogans that wouldn't offend anyone. They were about the right to say things that make people furious. Free speech means nothing unless it survives through the tough examples.

Why Limits on Speech Backfire

Every time the government tries to draw a broad line around "bad speech," it tends to overreach. Imagine that!

The Sedition Acts of 1798 were meant to silence a few critics but ended up fueling Jefferson's rise to power. The crackdowns during World War I made martyrs out of protesters like Eugene Debs. McCarthyism silenced artists and intellectuals but collapsed under its own excesses. If you look at the details of the death of McCarthyism, I think it's a classic example of how truth wins in the marketplace of ideas. It took a while to get there, but when it did, people felt kind of silly for supporting all those witch hunts.

The pattern is clear: censorship looks tempting in the moment, but usually ages very poorly, kind of like warm milk. Today's dangerous or unpopular idea might be tomorrow's necessary truth.

Free Speech and Personal Responsibility

One of the biggest takeaways in this whole discussion is how free speech is designed to be a shield against the government. It's not, and never was intended to be a "get out of jail free" card for offensive behavior. Just because you can say something doesn't mean it's wise, helpful, or kind. And it certainly doesn't mean you're free from consequences.

Living in a free society means pairing liberty with responsibility. That means fact-checking yourself, arguing in good faith, tolerating disagreement, and remembering that other people's right to speak is just as strong as yours, even if they're wrong! Liberty without maturity and a healthy dose of personal responsibility quickly implodes.

Your Toolkit for Judging Speech Issues

So, how do you apply all this in daily life? Here's a quick framework for evaluating any future speech controversy. I'll go ahead and bet you won't have to wait even a day to apply this.

1. Is the government involved? If not, it's probably not a First Amendment issue.
2. Does it fit into one of the narrow unprotected categories? (Incitement, true threats, defamation, obscenity, or fraud.)
3. Is it expression or action? (Breaking windows isn't speech, even if you yell a slogan while doing it.)
4. Is it just offensive or unpopular? If so, it's almost certainly protected.

With those four questions, you can cut through a lot of noise in the news cycle and figure out what's really at stake. And yes, even newscasters and talking heads can do a lousy

job of conflating real freedom of speech issues with unprotected behaviors.

Why It Still Matters Today

Democracy dies when we can no longer criticize the clowns
we elected to office.

The First Amendment doesn't just protect edgy comedi-
ans, angry protesters, or cranky bloggers. It protects everyone's ability to question authority, share ideas, and fight for
change. So, yes, democracies die when citizens lose the
ability to raise questions and poke holes. They thrive when
people can argue and even protest (peacefully) without fear.

Free speech is messy, noisy, and sometimes ugly. But
that's the sound of freedom hitting its stride.

The Founders didn't create the First Amendment to
make life comfortable. They created it to keep democracy
alive. Every time you hear a speech you hate, read an
opinion that makes you angry, or see a protest that drives
you nuts, just remember that's liberty in action.

The measure of our commitment isn't how we treat
speech we like. It's how we protect the voices we can't stand.
I recall a cheesy movie line from some years ago. I think the
film was *The American President*. The president was taking
political heat because his girlfriend or fiancée once burned
an American flag. He replied with something along these
lines:

"You want to claim this land as the land of the free?

Then the symbol of your country cannot just be a flag.

*The symbol also has to be one of its citizens exercising his
right to burn that flag in protest.*

*Now show me that, defend that, celebrate that in your
classrooms.*

Then you can stand up and sing about the land of the free."

I can't believe I just quoted a line from a corny movie, but you have to admit, it fits.

That's why the First Amendment, two centuries later, still matters more than ever.

EPILOGUE: YOUR FREEDOM, YOUR RESPONSIBILITY

The Founders gave us freedom of speech, but they also gave us an extraordinary gift: a government told to keep its hands off our voices, our beliefs, and our ideas. Keeping it alive is up to us. That means tolerating views we hate, arguing without fear, and remembering that liberty works best when it's messy.

But like any gift, it only matters if we use it. The First Amendment isn't a museum piece to admire behind glass; it's a tool meant to be handled, sometimes awkwardly, sometimes loudly, but always with purpose.

The Founders' Gift

When the Bill of Rights was ratified in 1791, it wasn't just an afterthought of a few forgotten ideas during the Constitutional Convention. It was a statement of trust: ordinary citizens, not kings or parliaments, would steer the future. That meant tolerating debate, dissent, and even harsh criticism. Benjamin Franklin put it bluntly when asked what kind of government the delegates had created: "A republic, if you can keep it."

Speech as a Civic Duty

The First Amendment isn't just a shield for individuals against potential government censorship or oppression. It also happens to be our collective job description. Democracy runs on participation. That means speaking up at town halls, writing letters, debating policy, sharing ideas, and yes, even posting online.

The marketplace of ideas works best when there's more than a couple of items on the shelf.

Silence may be safe, but it leaves the field open for those willing to shout the loudest. The silent majority never gets much done.

Tolerating What You Hate

Here's the hardest part: defending the rights of people whose views you despise. It's easy to champion free speech when you agree with it. That's kind of like saying you'll try any vegetable, as long as it's made of chocolate. It's much tougher when someone waves a flag you'd rather burn, makes a joke you find offensive, or campaigns for a cause you can't stand. You don't have to like it. All you have to do is recognize the other person's right to believe and say it.

Just remember, abolitionists, suffragists, and civil rights protesters all began as insufferable pains to the status quo. But protecting the unpopular is how we make sure tomorrow's breakthroughs have a chance to prove themselves.

Speech with Consequences

Remember: the First Amendment protects you from the government, not from consequences. If you say something outrageous, your neighbors can criticize you, your boss can discipline you, and your friends can uninvite you from their college football Saturday BBQ. That's not censorship. That's other people exercising their right to free speech.

Freedom doesn't mean immunity. It means everyone plays by the same rules.

Keeping the Conversation Alive

Reviewing all the cases noted in this book, you've probably noticed that free speech isn't something we define and defend once, then forget about. We constantly face new questions and tests with every world event, technological advance or societal trend. Whatever the underlying reason, the temptation to silence "dangerous" voices never goes away.

Your responsibility is to keep the conversation alive. That means questioning authority, tolerating disagreement, and remembering that democracy is noisy by design.

The moment debate goes silent, liberty starts to wither on the vine of freedom.

The Call to Action

You got this.

So here's the super condensed takeaway:

1. Speak boldly.
2. Listen generously.

3. Defend rights universally, not just for your side.

Free speech is like oxygen. You don't notice it until it's cut off, and by then, it's too late.

Protect it now, use it well, and it will keep this constitutional republic breathing freely.

The First Amendment isn't perfect, and neither are we. But together, they make possible the messy, argumentative, curious, innovative, and sometimes downright weird experiment called America.

Your freedom lives in your words. Use them wisely.

ABOUT THE AUTHOR

Tom has published about 10 books and a couple of thousand articles over the past decade or so while working as a magazine editor. He's the creator of Practical Guides—fun and lighter-side approaches to learning new things.

He finished college and his Master's of Business Administration degree about a hundred years ago. Before shifting gears and wading into the writing business, he spent a couple of decades in high-tech corporate marketing. Then he opened a restaurant, which was a really bad idea. He doesn't recommend it to anyone.

Tom is a voracious reader, having melted three Kindles so far, topically alternating between history, humor and well-written crime and suspense novels. Yeah, they're a great way to unwind.

You can find the latest at his website, and there's always a free eBook there for the taking, along with social media links if you'd like to connect.

tom-mchale.com

ALSO BY TOM MCHALE

The Practical Guide to America: Entertaining American History for Curious People

The Practical Guide to the United States Constitution

The Practical Guide to Becoming the Least Boring Person in the Room